PANZERWRECKS 16 INDEX

Vehicles

Tiger Ausf.B *36*
Tiger Ausf.E *2, 3, 38, 39*
Panther Ausf.G *inside front gatefold, 1, 40, 41, 42, 43, 48, 49, 73, 74, 75, 79, 95*
Panther Ausf.A *72*
Ersatz M10 *16, 17*
Jagdpanther *94, 96, inside rear gatefold*
Bergepanther *59, 60, 61*
Pz.Kpfw.IV Ausf.J *56, 57, 86*
Pz.Kpfw.IV Ausf.H *6, 7*
Pz.Kpfw.IV Ausf.G *5, 70, 71*
Pz.Bef.Wg. IV *87, 88, 89*
Panzer IV/70(V) *50, 51, 54, 55*
Jagdpanzer IV *52, 53*
Sturmgeschütz IV *8, 9, 12, 13*
Flakpanzer IV 'Wirbelwind' *4*
Hummel *90, 91*
Pz.Beob.Wg.III *37*
Sturmgeschütz III Ausf.G *10, 11, 14, 15, 59, 60, 61, 76, 77, 78, 79*
Bergepanzer III *93*
Jagdpanzer 38 *32, 93*
Grille Ausf.M *92*
s.P.S.W. (7·5cm) (Sd.Kfz.233) *80, 82, 83*
s.P.S.W. (5cm) (Sd.Kfz.234/2) *80*
kl.Pz.Fu.Wg. (Sd.kfz.261) *84*
m.S.P.W. (Sd.kfz.251) *32, 59, 61, 62, 69*
m.Fu.Pz.Wg. (Sd.Kfz.251/3) *84*
m.Kr.Pz.Wg. (Sd.Kfz.251/8) *44, 45*
m.S.P.W. (7·5cm K) (Sd.Kfz.251/9) *33*
m.S.P.W. (Drilling) (Sd.Kfz.251/21) *68*
Sf (Sd.Kfz.11/1) für 2cm Flak 38 auf le.ZgKw.3t *34*
m.Zgkw.8t (Sd.Kfz.7) *66, 67*
3·7cm Flak auf Sf. (Sd.Kfz.7/2) *rear gatefold*
s.W.S. *inside front gatefold, 63, 65*
Maultier *64*
le.Zgkw. 1t (Sd.Kfz.10) *85*
Sf für 2cm Flak 38 (Sd.Kfz.10/5) *85*
RSO/03 *32, 63*
RSO/01 *33*
M4 Sherman (captured) *18, 19, 20, 21, 22, 23, 24, 25*
M8 Light Armored Car *26, 27, 28, 29*
M2A1 Halftrack *30*
M3A1 Halftrack *31*
S.P.W. (Fu) auf Unic P 107 U 304(f) *47*
Muni-Zgkw auf Somua MCG S 307(f) *46*

Identified Locations

Belgium, Celles *80, 81, 82, 83, 84*
Belgium, Crombach *8*
Belgium, Faymonville *28, 29*
Belgium, Goronne *36*
Belgium, Grandmenil *74*
Belgium, Houffalize *37*
Belgium, La Falize *16, 17*
Belgium, Ligneuville *41*
Belgium, Neffe *26, 42, 43*
Belgium, Neufchâteau-Bastogne road *31*
Belgium, Ortho *46*
Belgium, Recogne *56, 57*
Belgium, Rocherath *55*
Belgium, Rochefort *94*
Belgium, St Vith *68*
Belgium, Verviers *69*
Luxembourg, Asselborn *67*
Luxembourg, Bourscheid *78, 79*
Luxembourg, Clervaux *10, 11*
Luxembourg, Dahl *95, 96, inside rear gatefold*

Luxembourg, Dasburg *58, 59, 60, 61, 62*
Luxembourg, Derenbach *44, 45*
Luxembourg, Esch-sur-Sûre *20, 21, 22, 23, 24*
Luxembourg, Eschdorf *12*
Luxembourg, Goesdorf to Heiderscheid road *70, 71*
Luxembourg, Hosingen *93*
Luxembourg, Kalborn *77*
Luxembourg, Kautenbach *66*
Luxembourg, Lullange *31*
Luxembourg, Marnach *48, 49, 50, 51, 52, 53*
Luxembourg, Michelau *33*
Luxembourg, Munshausen *14, 15*
Luxembourg, Oberwampach *38, 39*
Luxembourg, Rodershausen *inside front gatefold, 1, 2, 3, 4*
Luxembourg, Soller (Sonlez) *92*
Luxembourg, Wilwerdange *6, 7, 40*

Führer-Grenadier-Brigade *95*
Führer-Grenadier-Brigade, H.St.Art.Brig.911 *12, 14, 15*
Panzer-Lehr-Division, Pz.Lehr.Rgt.130 *inside front gatefold, 1, 42, 43*
Panzer-Lehr-Division, Pz.Gren.Lehr-Rgt.901 or 902 *92*
s.SS-Pz.Abt.501 *36*
s.Pz.Abt.506 *2, 3, 38, 39*
s.H.Pz.Jg.Abt.519 *96, inside rear gatefold*
SS-Vielfachwerfer-Batterie.522 *64*
s.H.Pz.Jg.Abt.559 *94*
s.H.Pz.Jg.Abt.560 *55*

Identified German Units

1.SS-Panzer-Division, SS-Pz.Rgt.1 *41*
1.SS-Panzer-Division, SS-Pz.Gren.Rgt.1 *69*
2.Panzer-Division *58, 59, 60, 61*
2.Panzer-Division, Pz.Rgt.3 *10, 11*
2.Panzer-Division, Pz.Aufkl.Abt.2 *80, 81, 82, 83, 84*
2.SS-Panzer-Division, SS-Pz.Rgt.2 *74*
2.SS-Panzer-Division, SS-Pz.Jg.Abt.2 *54*
3.Fallschirmjäger-Division *28, 29*
3.Panzergrenadier-Division, Pz.Abt.103 *77*
5.Fallschirmjäger-Division *18, 19, 20, 21, 22, 23, 24*
9.Panzer-Division, Pz.Rgt.33 *40, 48, 49, 56, 57, 86*
9.Panzer-Division, Pz.Art.Rgt.102 *37, 73*
12.Volksgrenadier-Division, Pz.Jg.Kp.1012a or 1012b *8*
15.Panzergrenadier-Division, Pz.Abt.115 *6, 7*
Panzer-Brigade 150 *16, 17*
Führer-Begleit-Brigade *44, 45, 70, 71, 78, 79*
Führer-Begleit-Brigade, StuG Abt.200 *46, 47*

A little closer to the Panther, which was assembled by Daimler-Benz in November 1944. It has the 'Balkenkreuz' in the middle of the hammer stowage brackets and early pattern idler wheels as used on Daimler-Benz Panthers throughout the war. A shell, perhaps from the Panther, has been wedged into the drive sprocket. Pz.Lehr.Rgt.130 was outfitted with Panthers in its 5. and 7. Kompanies during the 'Bulge'.

VDL(Bertogne)

During the Ardennes Offensive the only unit equipped with the Tiger I was 4./s.Pz.Abt.506. This example was left behind in Rodershausen and photographed by Pierre Bertogne and Tony Krier, Mr Krier's photo being taken on 29 March. The Tiger is unusual in that it has a late version commander's cupola with periscopes, but no visible 'Zimmerit' on the hull or gun mantlet. Spare track links on the driver's front plate afford a little extra protection, those between the driver's visor and ball MG being transport tracks. The building in the background is the same as shown in the gatefold, meaning that the Panther, Tiger and s.W.S. were in close proximity to each other.   **1x VDL(Bertogne), 1x VDL(Krier)**

A beaten-up Flakpanzer IV 'Wirbelwind' photographed in Rodershausen on 4 August 1945 by Tony Krier. In the valley below is the River Our, meaning that the vehicle was probably positioned here to cover the crossing further north at Dasburg. Putting a unit to it is a challenge, but contenders are s.Pz.Abt.506, St./Pz.Lehr.Rgt.130 or St./s.H.Pz.Jg.Abt.559. **VDL (Krier)**

A candidate for crew demolition. This rebuilt Pz.Kpfw.IV Ausf.G seems to have had a demolition charge set off in its engine compartment as the lower rear armour is cracked and deformed and the explosion has made a mess of the turret bin and 'Schürzen'. No details are available as to where or when it was taken, other than during the Ardennes Offensive. **NARA**

What a difference seven months made to this Pz.Kpfw.IV Ausf.H, photographed in Wilwerdange, Luxembourg. The image on the opposite page shows the vehicle as photographed by a US photographer in January 1945 where he says: *"A varied assortment of equipment & personal effects surrounding this German tank on a snowy Luxembourg road include such articles as women's coats, dresses, stockings, handbag, hats & other articles of feminine apparel."* The photo on this page was taken on 5 July 1945 by Tony Krier and shows how much of the vehicle has gone, no doubt including the women's clothes. The tank probably belonged to Pz.Abt.115 of 15.Panzergrenadier-Division who were in the area in mid January 1945. It is possible that this was originally a Pz.Brig.113 tank because Pz.Abt.115 took over about eight of their tanks in October 1944.   **1x NARA, 1x VDL(Krier)**

This Sturmgeschütz IV was photographed next to the church in Crombach, near Saint Vith, Belgium. The only units equipped with the Sturmgeschütz IV in the area were Pz.Jg. Kp.1012a and 1012b of 12.Volksgrenadier-Division. An unreadable chassis number has been painted on the (empty) roadwheel rack fixed to the side of the fighting compartment.
W.Auerbach

An armored bulldozer from the 305th Combat Engineer Battalion pushes a Sturmgeschütz IV, but to where? The StuG has a penetration through the fighting compartment rear armour, the resulting explosion blowing out the ventilator, leaving just the hole. A 'Flammentöter' muffler peeps out above the blade of the dozer. StuG IV units in the Ardennes were: Pz.Jg.Kp.1348 subordinated to 3.Fallschirmjäger-Division, Pz.Jg.Kp.1012a and 1012b with 12.Volksgrenadier-Division and Pz.Jg.Kp.1276 with 276.Volksgrenadier-Division. **L.Archer**

Rest in peace. Sturmgeschütz III Ausf.G, tactical number '523', of 5./Pz.Rgt.3, 2.Panzer-Division and an M4A3 of 707th Tank Battalion have ended their days in Clervaux cemetery. The 5. and 6./Pz.Rgt.3 were equipped with StuG III, whereas the 7. and 8./Pz.Rgt.3 were outfitted with Pz.Kpfw.IV. The photo on the opposite page was taken by PFC Joseph Lapine on 11 February 1945 and shows that the driver of the M4A3 was T/4 Hiar, as stencilled on the glacis plate. The two photos above were taken several months later where details emerge, such as the tactical number and 2.Panzer-Division's trident emblem on the bow of the Sturmgeschütz. **Bottom right:** Destruction within as portrayed by PFC Lapine.

1x NARA, 1x L.Archer, 1x MNHM(Krier), 1x USAHEC

A dejected looking Sturmgeschütz III Ausf.G photographed in Eschdorf, Luxembourg on 14 May 1945. According to the unit insignia on the bow, this StuG belonged to H.St.Art. Brig.911/Führer-Grenadier-Brigade. An explosion has blown the roof off the fighting compartment and rotated the gun barrel within its mantlet. Note the mounts for spare roadwheels on the track guards and scars from small arms fire on the bow armour.

MNHM(Krier)

This Sturmgeschütz III has the look of a vehicle that has had demolition charges set off. The engine deck and superstructure roof have been blown off, and a charge in the gun barrel has left it severed on the ground in front of the vehicle. Photographed by Tony Krier on 11 April 1945 and captioned by him as both Marnach and Munshausen. **VDL(Krier)**

Above and opposite top: More of Tony Krier's photos from 11 April 1945, these taken in Munshausen. Workshop crews had to be mindful that whatever modifications they made to a vehicle would not interfere with the operation of existing hatches and tool stowage or obstruct vision. The photo on this page provides a good view of the underside of the engine hatch cooling louvres. Note the pivoting hatch for the hole for the starting crank is missing, the unusual placement of the rear 'Balkenkreuz' and the relocated spare roadwheel mounts on the rear 'frame'. **Opposite bottom:** Tony Krier revisited the wreck in 1946 and much had disappeared. This may be another StuG from H.St.Art.Brig.911/Fhr. Gren.Brig. On 15 January 1945 the brigade was located a few kilometers to the southwest of Munshausen in the Drauffelt - Eschweiler area. **2x MNHM(Krier), 2x VDL(Krier)**

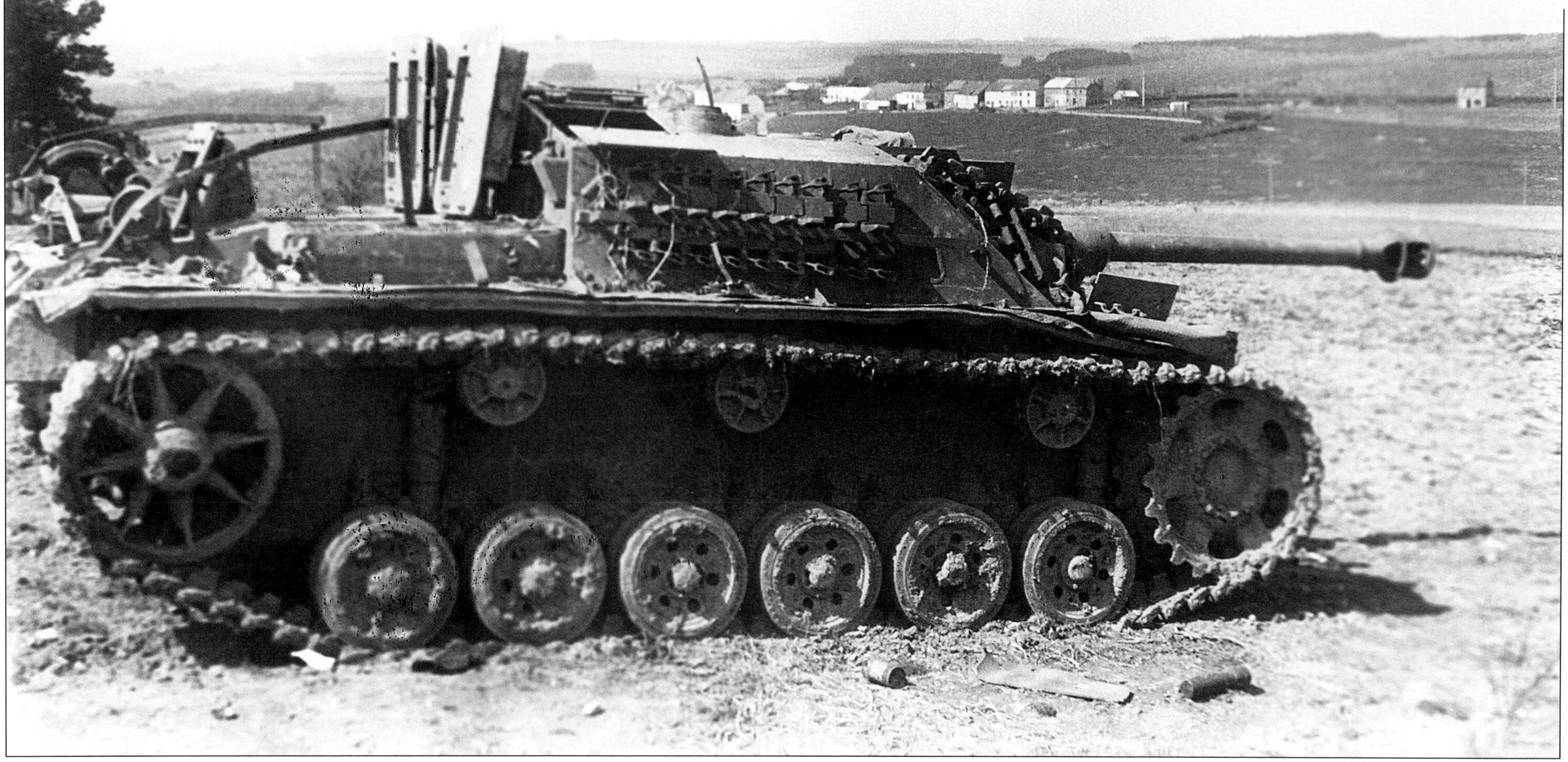

Alle Räder stehen
Still

Still

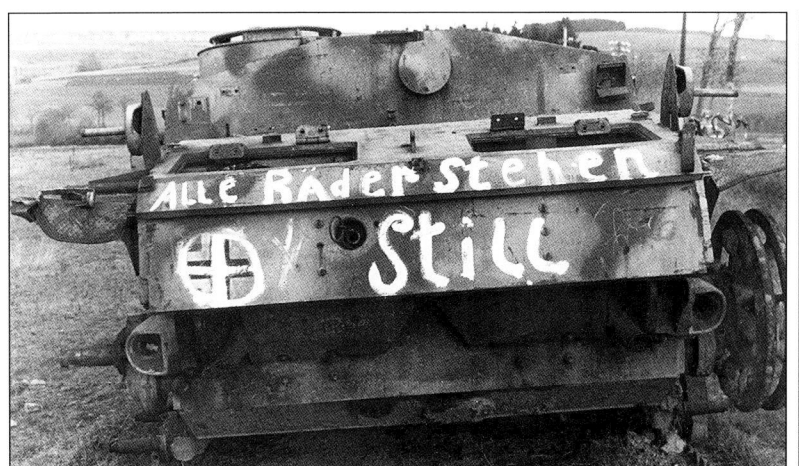

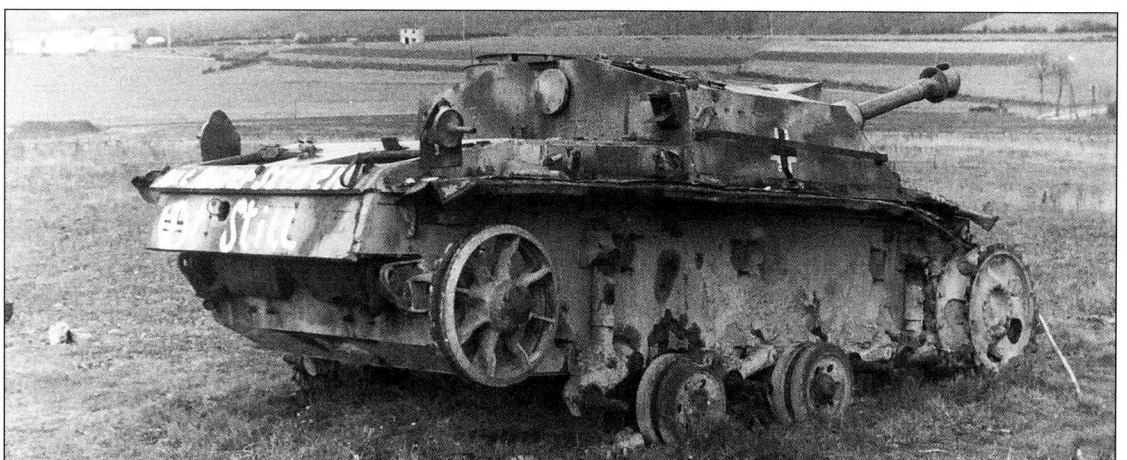

Subterfuge - Allied or German?

This 'Panther' is no stranger to our books, being on pages 39-41 of Panzerwrecks 4. Roddy MacDougall takes up its story: *"The Panther was one of five new vehicles converted by M·A·N in November 1944 for operation 'Rabenhugel' where it was disguised with sheet metal panels to resemble a US M10 tank destroyer. It was given the bumper code B10 along with other markings that it was hoped would pass any cursory examination if it encountered Allied troops during its original mission. It never fulfilled its intended role and was used in a conventional attack as part of Kampfgruppe X on Malmedy on 21st December 1944. It was knocked out at La Falize where it was backed into the café."*

L.Archer

Timm Haasler tells us a bit more: *"Panther B10, Leutnant Gerstenschläger, left behind on 21/12/44 at the Café Du Rocher de Falize. Due to the lack of the commander's cupola, Lt. Gerstenschläger was hit in his forehead when he peered out of the turret in order to orientate himself. He died the same day from this wound. Taken over by Olt. Dreier the tank crew received the order to move back when the Kampfgruppe abandoned the battlefield in front of Malmedy the same day. The tank started to move when it came under heavy American artillery fire. The driver tried to escape from this threat by moving back, but ran into the cafe. The crew abandoned the tank and ran away."*

L.Archer

Subterfuge - Allied or German?

What is probably a wrecking crew breaking up the detritus of war for scrap. The detritus in question is most likely one of six M4A3s captured by the 5.Fallschirmjäger-Division at Wiltz in December 1944. At least six shells have penetrated the Sherman's turret, and a couple have glanced off the top. Captured tanks often had more than their fair share of 'Balkenkreuze' painted onto them, this vehicle being no exception with them on the hull side, glacis plate, turret side and turret top. The camouflage pattern is reminiscent of the 9th Armored Division's scheme. At least one other Sherman is in the background, its Allied star peering out from the engine deck of the captured vehicle.

W.Auerbach

Subterfuge - Allied or German?

Above: What we think is another of 5.Fallschirmjäger-Division's Shermans among the long grass. It carries fewer 'Balkenkreuze' than the vehicle on the opposite page, but they are much larger and the example on the hull side has been applied around what appears to be the name that the US crew applied. **Right:** From the same collection as the previous two captured M4s, this one has 'Swastikas' instead of 'Balkenkreuze', the one on the gun mantlet being an interesting choice of position. The US registration number at the rear of the hull side has been painted over.

2x W.Auerbach

Subterfuge - Allied or German?

Subterfuge - Allied or German?

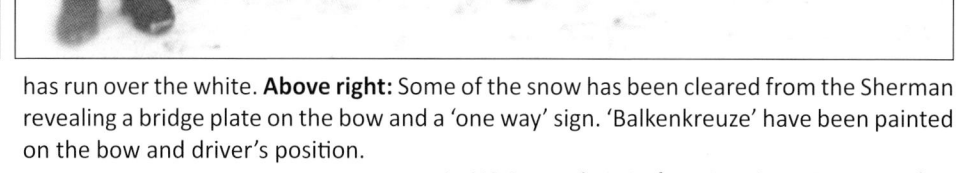

Opposite and above left: A well known 'Beutepanzer.' The best known of the six Shermans captured by 5 Fallschirmjäger Division in Wiltz. Here we see it abandoned outside the Hotel des Ardennes in Esch-sur-Sûre on 24 January 1945 as photographed by a US Signal Corps photographer. The close-up photo shows how the black paint of the 'Balkenkreuz' has run over the white. **Above right:** Some of the snow has been cleared from the Sherman revealing a bridge plate on the bow and a 'one way' sign. 'Balkenkreuze' have been painted on the bow and driver's position.

1x US Army via L.Archer, 1x USAHEC, 1x L.Archer

Subterfuge – Allied or German?

Above: The tank was photographed by Tony Krier on 28 April 1945. The bow armour and gearbox, complete with drive sprockets, have been removed making the tank look more like an empty shell than a fighting vehicle. The placement of the tank next to the Hotel des Ardennes would have provided cover for one of the bridges across the river Sûre. **Right:** An overhead view shows that the Sherman still had an Allied star on the turret roof.

2x VDL (Krier)

Subterfuge - Allied or German?

Subterfuge - Allied or German?

T/5 Tony Brichta of 728th Maintenance Company poses with the wrecked Sherman. With the turret traversed to the left we can see that the rack visible on the rear of the turret on pages 20-21 has been removed. In the background is the bank of the river Sûre.

W.Brichta

An M4A3 of 3rd Tank Battalion, 10th Armored Division that had been captured by German forces earlier in the offensive. Unusually for a 'Beutepanzer' it does not have prevalent 'Balkenkreuze' as shown on preceding pages, just a solitary cross on a white background on the glacis plate. The Allied stars on the hull sides have been painted over. It was photographed on 6 February 1945, but we don't know if the Germans used it with or without the turret. **1x NARA, 1x USAHEC**

Subterfuge - Allied or German?

Subterfuge - Allied or German?

Opposite: S/Sgt Charles W. Griffin stares at markings of the last owner of an M8 Light Armored Car, which apparently had been captured several weeks before the start of the Ardennes Offensive. The photograph was taken on the road leading to Neffe, Belgium on 15 January 1945.

USAHEC

This page: Another captured M8. There is an outside possibility that this could be the same vehicle as seen on the opposite page, but the serial number is too faint on the opposite page to tell. It is also difficult to tell what colour the 'Balkenkreuz' is, as it appears darker than the white of the Allied star; note how the legs of the 'Balkenkreuz' and the middle of the star are painted onto the turret rail. Being a scan from a well focussed and exposed negative, details such as the writing on the tyre walls become visible.

L.Archer

Subterfuge - Allied or German?

Subterfuge - Allied or German?

The 3.Fallschirmjäger-Division captured this M8 Light Armored Car in the Losheim Gap at the start of the offensive and lost it at Faymonville church on 18 January 1945. The caption for the photograph credits the US 1st Infantry Division with capturing it. Note the 'Swastika' covering an Allied star on the rear fender. **3x NARA**

Subterfuge - Allied or German?

Subterfuge - Allied or German?

A rather gaunt soldier stands before an M2A1 halftrack with the bumper code for 1st Army, 275th Armored Field Artillery Bn. which was an independent unit attached to the 7th AD just as the battle for St. Vith was shaping up. The 275th helped stave off several heavy German attacks but succumbed to a German artillery concentration themselves and got knocked out of St. Vith around 21 December or so, but not before winning a Presidential unit citation. Transport-starved troops from Volksgrenadier divisions and other units eagerly grabbed up whatever American vehicles were still serviceable, and an AFA Bn had 32 of the M3A1 halftracks listed in their TO&E.

W. Auerbach

An M3 or M3A1 halftrack with remarkably neat 'Balkenkreuz' on the side and rear door was abandoned near Lullange, Luxembourg, and photographed by a US Signal Corps photographer on 3 February 1945. The bumper markings say 9th Armored Division, 52nd Armored Infantry Battalion. During mid-December, 1944, components of the division were located in Luxembourg, Belgium and France as they sought to recover from the initial German assault on 16 December 16th; CCB in Saint Vith, CCA near Emsdorf and CCR in Bastogne.

USAHEC

Subterfuge – Allied or German?

An M3A1 halftrack lies in a ditch on the road between Neufchâteau and Bastogne on 29 December 1944. The original is a wirephoto, a method of transmitting photographs by telephone, the trade-off being that there was a significant drop in quality. A careful look at the side of the halftrack shows a 'Swastika' painted alongside the Allied star.

L.Archer

Subterfuge – Allied or German?

The caption says: *"An American Military Policeman points to a single star, insignia of the Allied forces, on a German halftrack captured in the Ardennes salient in Belgium."* But was it used by German or US forces? This is a radiophoto hence its slightly 'jaggy' look. The signpost behind the m.S.P.W. has been censored.

L.Archer

The 'Howell Mission,' possibly named for the 82nd Airborne's Brig. Gen George P. Howell, visited the Ardennes for a short period of time in the winter of 1945. Very little is known about the reason for this mission, and only a handful of photographs testify to its existence. These are seen above, on page 34 and at the bottom of page 63. **Above:** This m.S.P.W. (7·5cm Kanone) (Sd.Kfz.251/9) Ausf.D has a tactical sign on its rear plate. **NARA**

Opposite top: On the left we see a Selbstfahrlafette (Sd.Kfz.11/1) für 2cm Flak 38 auf le.ZgKw.3 t mit Panzerschutz (minus its weapon) and on the right a whitewashed Jagdpanzer 38 straddles the shoulder of the road. The former was covered by ETO Technical Intelligence Report No. 151 'German Semi-Tracked Cargo Vehicle,' dated 11 February 1945, where it was noted as having a Luftwaffe licence plate. **Opposite bottom:** Two views of the RSO/03.

3x NARA

This page: An RSO/01 photographed in Michelau, Luxembourg on 3 August 1945. The lower photo shows that the rear of the cab has been painted with five small white stars, these do not appear anywhere else on the vehicle leading us to conclude that it was probably not used by Allied forces.

2x VDL(Krier)

Lt. Seum, 486th AAA Battalion (SP), 3rd Armored Division, photographed this Tiger II "*at Malmedy*" in January 1945, saying in his caption that it had been 'booby-trapped'. The tank, from 3./s.SS-Pz.Abt.501, was lost at Goronne on 7 January 1945 while supporting I./Gren.Rgt.753. More information and photos of this Tiger can be found in *Duel in the Mist 3*.
L.Archer

The 9.Panzer-Division (note the insignia on the driver's front plate) left this Pz.Beob.Wg.III looking down Rue Ville-Basse in Houffalize where it was photographed by a US Airforce photographer, a GI, and townsfolk alike. It is surprising how much these heavy vehicles were moved around after their capture or destruction. In this instance it has been rotated, then moved to another street. Apparently Pz.Art.Rgt.102 (9.Pz.Div.) lost all three of its Pz.Beob.Wg.III during January 1945.

3x L.Archer, 1x NARA

S/Sgt Glenn Keller and PFC Virgil McWilliams, mortar observers from D Company, 358th Infantry Regiment, 90th Infantry Division in front of a snow covered Tiger I near Oberwampach, Luxembourg on 21 January 1945.

NARA

With the snow now gone details emerge, such as the tactical number '411', scar at the top of the driver's front plate next to the radio operator's position and damaged muzzle brake. The Tiger has steel wheels fitted, although the outer wheels have been removed. The only unit equipped with the Tiger I in the 'Bulge' was 4./s.H.Pz.Abt.506. **L.Archer**

The winch cable of an M32B1 recovery vehicle has been hitched to this Befehlspanther of II./Pz.Rgt.33, 9.Panzer-Division at Wilwerdange, Luxembourg, the same vehicle as shown on page 83 of Panzerwrecks 1. The inset photo, taken on 5 July 1945, shows that the recovery effort was unsuccessful. The Panther was assembled by M·A·N in late September or October 1944 and was fitted with a strengthened mantlet.

1x L.Archer, 1x VDL(Krier)

Locals inspect the wreck of Panther '152' outside Hotel des Ardennes in Ligneuville, Belgium in 1946. The man in the middle is pointing at the shell hole in the side armour of the Panther, which has set off an explosion inside; note how the bottom of the sponson has been bowed. The tank is unusual in that the turret has a 'Zimmerit' coating, but the hull does not. **Inset:** Air liaison officers with the wreck on 3 February 1945. The Panther belonged to Stab of I./SS-Pz.Rgt.1 and was commanded by Ustuf. Arndt Fischer when it was knocked out in the afternoon of 17 December 1944. **1x L.Archer, 1x NARA**

Opposite: The end of the Panzer Lehr's advance into Neffe. Two Panthers are shown here on the Rue de Clervaux; the lead vehicle (assembled by M.N.H.) is missing the starboard track after hitting a mine, the following vehicle (assembled by Daimler-Benz) was hit in the side several times by a tank or anti tank gun. The GI in the bottom photos, taken on 3 January 1945, is from the 6th Armored Division. **This page:** Time and snow has moved on revealing the rear Panther has been completely overturned and stripped, while the lead Panther slowly loses its wheels and tracks. The turret number of the lead vehicle is '533', making it a vehicle from 5./Pz.Rgt.130.

4x USAHEC, 2x L.Archer

Opposite: A mittlerer Krankenpanzerwagen (Sd.Kfz.251/8) Ausf.D from Führer-Begleit-Brigade (note the well defined insignia on the nose) gets the once over by a GI, presumably an engineer with a bridging unit. He may be assessing the possibility of using the 6-ton 6x6 Bridge Erector Truck to haul away the wreck. **This page:** One wonders what caused the hull-splitting explosion and fire, but rocket firing aircraft, artillery and tank fire could all do the trick. Note the effects of shell fire on the wall in the background. Although captioned Brachtenbach, Timm Haasler identified the location as Derenbach where Führer-Begleit-Brigade and about 10 Tigers of 9.Panzer-Division (s.H.Pz.Abt.506) fought a rearguard action between 19 and 21 January 1945. Führer-Begleit-Brigade was commanded by Ernst Otto Remer who received command of the unit as a reward for his part in crushing operation Valkyrie, the plot to assassinate Hitler in July 1944.

2x L.Archer

Sturmgeschütz Abteilung 200, part of Führer-Begleit-Brigade during the Ardennes Offensive, left this Munitions-Zugkraftwagen, gepanzert auf Somua MCG S 307(f) in Ortho, Belgium. The large 'M' on the side wall stands for 'Munition', and part of its load is strewn around the rear of the vehicle. Although worn, the crew have been careful to avoid whitewashing over the unit insignia and 'M' on the side. As a survivor of the Normandy maelstrom it is missing a few bits and pieces, notably the front tow hooks, headlamp and some of the armoured radiator louvres.

IWM

Another of Sturmgeschütz Abteilung 200's Normandy survivors, this one a Schützenpanzerwagen (Funk) auf Unic P 107 U 304(f). It was the subject of a US Army Tech Intell report who described it as: *"A German armored vehicle built on a French [Unic] half-track chassis ... encountered in the Third US Army area. Both the driver and assistant driver are provided with two vision ports with hinged flaps. Entrance is through an opening in the rear. A large hatch is provided in the top of the body. Two half doors are hinged at the outer edge. Two studs are welded to the top. A seat runs the entire length of the left side. Three antenna bases were installed on the top of the vehicle, one at the right rear and one on each side toward the front of the compartment."* **3x NARA**

Mangled at Marnach

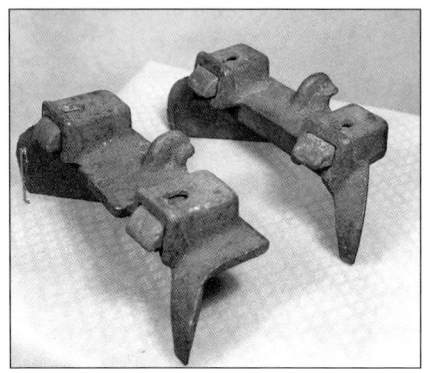

Above: Two Panthers destroyed beside a copse outside Marnach, on the road to Dasburg during their retreat from the 'Bulge'. The tank in the foreground carries a small tactical number '701', indicative of 7./Pz.Rgt.33 of 9.Panzer-Division. **Left:** Many Panthers in the offensive were fitted with 'Mittelstollen', seen here during evaluation by the Allies, early version at the top, late version below.

1x USAHEC, 3x NARA

Mangled at Marnach

The Panther seen in the background of the previous page. The explosion that blew the turret from the hull also took away the hull side and the driver's roof armour. The tank had been fitted with 'Mittelstollen' as seen on the previous page, and overpainted with whitewash, much of which remains on the glacis plate.

NARA

Mangled at Marnach

Only a few metres from the Panthers lies this Panzer IV/70(V), the result of a direct hit by an aerial bomb. The explosion was so powerful that the sides and roof of the fighting compartment are nowhere to be seen, but unexploded ammunition is strewn on both sides of the wreck. In the background is the copse where the two Panthers lie. B-26s of the 9th Airforce bombed the German forces retreating to the river Our on 22 January 1945.

1x USAHEC, 1x NARA

Mangled at Marnach

Mangled at Marnach

A few hundred metres from the Panzer IV/70(V) and two Panthers lies this Jagdpanzer IV with a broken back, courtesy of an aerial bomb or demolition charges The vehicle is clad with a full coat of 'Zimmerit' and has three kill rings painted around the end of the gun barrel. In the background is a wrecked 7·5cm Pak 40. **Right:** Pvt. W. E. Hansel peers inside.
1x USAHEC, 1x NARA

Mangled at Marnach

Panzer IV/70(V), tactical number '214' menacingly points its nose out from a pine wood. It bears the scars of battle; a chunk out of the lower side of the gun mantlet and one on the top corner, which glanced off the mantlet and glacis plate; the corrosion around these helps to define them. Although not a particularly clear photo, the casting numbers are visible on the side of the gun mount and mantlet. The vehicle, from 2./SS-Pz.Jg.Abt.2, was destroyed on 6 January 1945 between Belle Haie and Baraque Fraiture while supporting SS-Pz.Aufkl.Abt.2 defend the cross-roads against elements of 3rd Armored Division. During the Ardennes Offensive SS-Pz.Jg.Abt.2 was attached to SS-Pz.Aufkl.Abt.2. **L.Archer**

This mud-smeared Panzer IV/70(V) was one of two lost by 3./s.H.Pz.Jg.Abt.560 in Rocherath during the night of 18/19 December 1944, quite possibly succumbing to tanks of the 741st Tank Battalion. Note the cut out mantlet flange and shredded end of gun barrel. To the right of the Panzer IV/70(V) is a Panther from SS-Pz.Rgt.12. The photograph was taken by T/4 Paul J. Ott from Co.D 741st Tank Battalion. **Above:** The emblem on the side of the mantlet is 'Kohlenklau,' which translates as 'coal thief'.

1x R.Ott via M.Krawczyk, 1x L.Archer

The American AP rounds flying around in December 1944 were different from those used six months earlier, and the crews of Panzer IVs were probably aware that their frontal armour could not only be penetrated, but shattered off in chunks. And still they sallied forth to support the attack. From the degree of scorching present, this Pz.Kpfw.IV Ausf.J, knocked out in Recogne, Belgium, must have burnt like a funeral pyre. The tank, tactical number '322' of I./Pz.Rgt.33, was assembled in September 1944 and destroyed on 13 January 1945.

2x USAHEC, 1x J.Tomkinson

The chaotic scene on the west bank of the Our River looking east to Germany resembles the aftermath of a tornado. Engineers are working on a replacement for the Dasburger Brücke, a bridge built in 1846 connecting Luxembourg and Germany. It was jammed with German vehicles on both sides when American bombers visited on 22 January 1945. A GI peers into the bowels of a Pz.Kpfw.IV chassis. **Opposite:** There are two Demag assembled Bergepanthers in the debris at Dasburg. The unit was probably 2.Panzer-Division. **L.Archer**

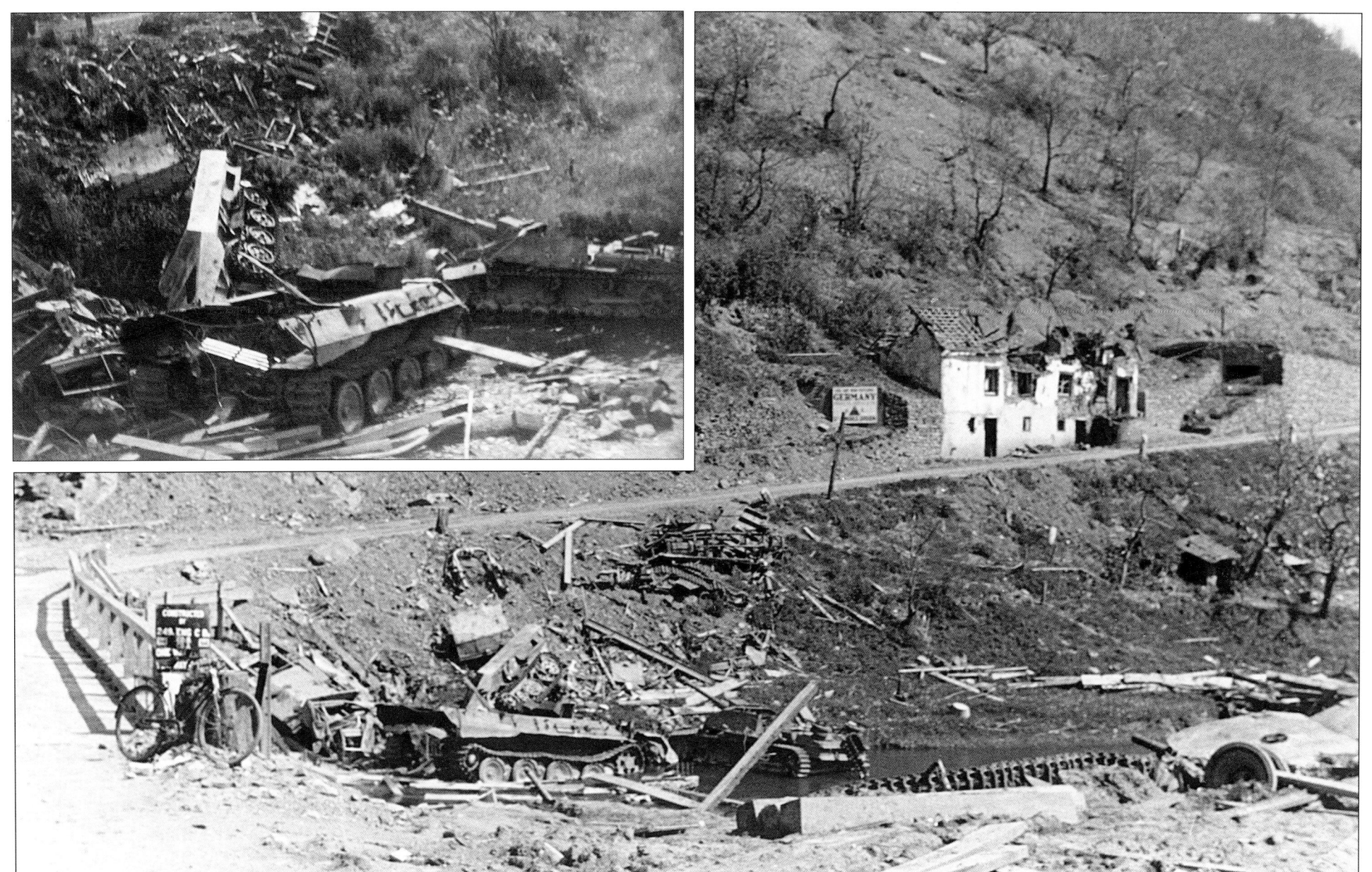

West bank looking east. On a sunny day later in 1945 the effects of the bombing seem preordained, but that was hardly the case a few months earlier. As recounted by Oak Mackey in the Winter 2006 issue of *The Second Air Division Assn JOURNAL:* Mission #226 of 10Jan45, Target: Dasburg, began as follows: *The weather was absolutely atrocious - through the night there had been a combination of freezing rain, sleet, snow showers and fog. The runways and taxiways were covered with a sheet of slippery ice. Our assigned plane had not been warmed up, the engines were cold and very difficult to start.* Once airborne: *#3 engine propeller severely over-speeded, probably because of congealed oil trying to pass through the propeller governor. This is a serious problem - because the over-speeded engine might turn to junk, or the propeller might come off the engine and pass through the fuselage or hit the other engine on that side. With one engine out and a loaded airplane, there was no way we could stay with the Group.* **1x VDL(Krier), 1x W.Auerbach**

Low tide for the Wehrmacht as even a retrograde movement meant destruction of their vehicles. Whatever 'General Purpose' bombs dropped from planes did not destroy, a tumble down a riverbank surely wrecked. Here a Sturmgeschütz III Ausf.G and a Bergepanther have lost entire chunks of their armour. The Bergepanther's winch lies on the waters edge, the cables snaking back into the vehicle. Note in the upper left of the photo, a pillbox built into the wall which provided MG cover for the bridge. Full details of the Bergepanther can be found in *Panzer Tracts* 16-1. The 9th Armored Infantry Battalion took Dasburg on 21 February 1945.
NARA

On the east bank looking west to Luxembourg. Parts of a m.S.P.W. (Sd.Kfz.251) and a second Bergepanther can be seen under the trestle bridge. Wrecks stayed there after the bridge was replaced, note that the Pz.Kpfw.IV chassis is still in position next to the building on the right.

2x L.Archer

These two m.S.P.W. (Sd.Kfz.251) are captioned as being knocked out by the US 6th Armored Division near Dasburg and awaiting removal from the side of the road. It looks to us as if they have already been pushed and judging from the track marks on the slope behind it, the SPW on the left may have remained upright, and the one on the right may have reversed down the slope.

NARA

s.W.S. stripped. It looks as if this s.W.S. was seeking shelter in a barn before its destruction. The load-bed is missing and the front end has had an impact or explosion. The first road wheel reached the extreme limits of travel on its swing arm, apparently without breaking the track. It is captioned as Heinerscheid or Marnach, Luxembourg 30 March 1945.
VDL(Krier)

Another photo taken by the Howell Mission. Depicted are the snow covered remains of an RSO/03 (Diesel) and a s.W.S. While each was designed as a prime mover/artillery tractor, they were worlds apart in terms of performance:

	RSO	s.W.S.
Towing capacity:	3000kg	8000kg
Payload:	1500kg	4000kg
Top speed:	14·5km/hr	27·4/18·3km/hr

The supply of Argus brakes was a bottleneck in the production of both vehicles.

NARA

Heinerscheid, Marnach, or between the two, Luxembourg, 30 March 1945. A 'Maultier' has lost part of its load of 8cm 'Raketensprenggranate', ammunition for the 8cm 'Vielfachwerfer.' This launcher could fire 48 rockets in a very short period of time and was a copy of the Russian Katyusha launcher for the Russian M8 rocket. As far as we know the only unit equipped with the Vielfach-Panzerwerfer during the offensive was SS-Vielfachwerfer-Batterie.522, attached to 6.Panzer-Armee.

VDL (Krier)

A schwerer Wehrmachts-Schlepper (s.W.S.) knocked out in Luxembourg. The running gear is missing some roadwheels, one has come away from its hub, and the front wheels are also nowhere to be seen. It had been carrying a supply of ammunition in individual 'luftdichter Patronenkasten' some of which are strewn around the wreck. The aft section of the load bed would have been fitted with wooden benches for the crew, with the fence-like structure in this example supporting a rifle rack for their weapons. **MNHM**

Three boys pose with 'Ilse', a mittlerer Zugkraftwagen 8t (Sd.Kfz.7) left behind in Kautenbach, Luxembourg. Considering the lack of fittings on the load bed, we think that the vehicle was a load carrier rather than a Flakwagen. It seems that front and outer roadwheels were of more use to the locals than the 'Allwetterverdeck' (canvas cover) over the cab which remains, albeit battered.

VDL(Bertogne)

90th Division infantrymen and tankers inspect a m.Zgkw. 8 ton 'Holzpritschenaufbau mit Holzfahrerhaus,' (a prime mover with a wooden driver's cab and load bed) that had been blown up by a German mine. In everyone's mind, it may have simply registered as 'one less.' This Zugkraftwagen was the tow vehicle for the infamous '88,' and perhaps they remember that gun's handiwork on their own vehicles. Asselborn, Luxembourg 22 January 1945. The 9th Armored Infantry Battalion shown on the sign belonged to the 6th Armored Division.
US Army via L.Archer

A mittlerer Schützenpanzerwagen (Drilling) (Sd.Kfz.251/21), apparently photographed in St Vith, where civilians peer into the fighting compartment. The triple barrelled mount is trained to the 9 o'clock position, with the butts of the 'überschwer' MGs on the left in the photo. Apart from the drive sprocket, all the wheels have been removed. Unit insignias were often painted on the nose armour of SPWs, but unfortunately not on this example.

L.Archer

The unit insignia on the side of this mittlerer Schützenpanzerwagen (Sd.Kfz.251) is the same as that on page 26 of Panzerwrecks 2, making it a SS-Pz.Gren.Rgt.1 survivor from Normandy. This is confirmed by the partial insignia on the rear door. Here Clarence Nelson from '1st Army' poses in the halftrack in Verviers, Belgium, December 1944. **L.Archer**

Above: Precariously perched on the side of the road from Goesdorf to Heiderscheid is this Pz.Kpfw.IV from III./Führer-Grenadier-Brigade, and had previously belonged to Pz.Gren. Brig von Werthern. The tank was destroyed while defending the Dahl plateau on 7 January 1945, here Cpl Ramon L. McCraw, PFC Floyd Wells and Pvt Bobby Robinson investigate on 10 January. **Opposite:** With the snow gone a few details emerge, such as the chassis number '82339' painted under the tow point, rounded muzzle brake, differing 'Zimmerit' patterns on the brake access hatches and driver's front plate, and the welded-on rod next to the driver's vision port which presumably held spare track links. Although the chassis number would point to an Ausf.F, making it truly an 'old hare,' Hilary Doyle explains that *"... In the few situations where we have detailed records of the deliveries from assembly firms we find that the Fahrgestell Nr can only be used as a general guideline: It should be an Ausf.F (7,5cm Kw.K.L/24) assembled by Krupp about January 1942. It would have been about 120 vehicles before the introduction of extra armour.* [Continued on next page.]
NARA

The characteristics, however, are all those of an early Ausf G. **Original features:** Starting in May 1942, sixteen Ausf.G had nose armour 50mm welded in place, but cut to permit the use of the KFF2 over the driver's visor. I strongly doubt that this type of armour upgrade would have been undertaken during a rebuild. The KFF was plugged from February 1943 so any adding of armour after that date would not have the cut out. Deflector on mantlet shows the antenna has not yet been moved to the rear (May 1943). Visor on right side of turret was eliminated in April 1942 but was still present on some early Ausf.G. **Rebuild features:** The gun appears to be L/48 and as these did not appear until April 1943 it would have to be part of a rebuild. The same is true for the Schürzen (April 1943). Zimmerit only appeared in January 1944 so is definitely part of a rebuild. My opinion is that '82339' was one of the earliest Pz.Kpfw.IV fitted with the extra armour and the Fahrgestell is a straggler from the Ausf.F that actually was completed in April-May 42 as an Ausf.F2 (Ausf.G.) Then it was backfitted with Schürzen and Zimmerit during later rebuilds." Our thanks to Hilary for this detailed information.

L.Archer

An unusual sight in the 'Bulge' is this Panther Ausf.A that has taken a round into the hull side and another lower down in the running gear. It would seem that the ammunition cooked off as the bottom of the sponson, where the ammunition was stowed, has deformed. Note the missing idler wheel and spiked gun barrel with its peeling banana appearance? A GI, perhaps the photographer, leaned his M-1 carbine against the front of the track. Putting a unit to this tank is difficult as there is no caption and no markings other than a faint 'Balkenkreuz'.

NARA

A battle-scarred Panther Ausf.G with five kill-rings on the gun barrel. Putting a unit ID to this wreck is tough as there is no caption, but Timm Haasler shares his knowledge: *"These kill rings had become a rare sight in December 1944/January 1945. For sure this was the tank of a veteran. As all Waffen-SS units received a full set of new tanks after Normandy and had their first engagement after the retreat from France in December 44/January 45 we can exclude 1., 2., 9., and 12.SS-Pz.Rgt. 2. Pz.Div. and Pz.Lehr Div. also received new tanks after Normandy, but Pz.Rgt. 3 wasn't engaged between October and December in the West. 9. Pz.Div. and 116. Pz.Div. stayed in combat even after Normandy, receiving several tanks from the depots and incorporating Panzer brigades. So these kill rings were earned during the engagements on the Western Front between September and December 1944. So my guess, this is a former tank from Pz.Rgt. 16, 33 or 130. A couple of weeks ago I came across a very interesting statement provided by a former tank driver of Pz.Rgt. 33. He stated that after they managed to return their Panther back to Germany after the engagement in the Ardennes, they used the time before the next second engagement during the Bulge to paint newly earned kill rings to their gun. It is obvious that Pz.Rgt. 33 continued the tradition of painting kill rings onto the gun for each enemy tank they managed to destroy. As this is the only Panther I know of which is showing kill rings during the Bulge, and the information provided by a veteran of Pz.Rgt. 33, I guess this is tank was a former tank of Pz.Rgt. 33 - just my two cents."* Thanks Timm!

L.Archer

One of 13 Panthers from I./SS-Pz.Rgt.2, 2.SS.Panzer-Division knocked out in and around Grandmenil on 24 December 1944 during an engagement against M10s from the 628th Tank Destroyer Battalion and troops from 238th Engineers and 75th Infantry Division. The Panther was assembled by M·A·N. in October or early November 1944.

L.Archer

A November or early December production Daimler-Benz Panther Ausf.G has been pushed off the road. The camouflage net does a reasonable job of obscuring the details of the tank; good for the crew, but not much help for us trying to piece together the history of the tank. No tactical number is visible on the turret side. **L.Archer**

A very sorry looking Sturmgeschütz III Ausf.G from an unidentified unit lies in a snowy field. The gun barrel has been spiked by the crew or the Americans, to prevent its reuse and the roof of the fighting compartment is missing, which indicates that demolition charges were probably placed in there too. Heavy damage to the drive sprocket and mudguard could mean that the vehicle hit a mine, disabling it. Note the two armour piercing projectiles sitting on the mudguard.

L.Archer

The method of displaying the tactical number on this Sturmgeschütz III Ausf.G is unique to Pz.Abt.103, 3.Panzergrenadier-Division. We have published photos of their wrecks while fighting in Italy; in Panzerwrecks 9 and 13. This example was photographed in Kalborn, Luxembourg. The roof is missing and the gun is dislodged, as indicated by the muzzle brake in front of drive sprocket. Note how the hubs are missing from two of the three return rollers and the remaining roadwheel.

L.Archer

This seemingly intact Sturmgeschütz III Ausf.G has run into, or been abandoned by, a wrecked building in Bourscheid, Luxembourg. The vehicle, which has its superstructure front clad in spare track, has a tactical number of '542' painted onto the side of the cast gun mantlet. It belonged to Führer-Grenadier-Brigade who also left behind a Panther and RSO in Bourscheid between 24 and 26 December 1944.

MNHM

Top left: A Führer-Grenadier-Brigade Panther left behind in Bourscheid and photographed on 12 July 1945 by Tony Krier. The tank, an Ausf.G assembled by M·A·N, has a broken starboard track and 'Zimmerit' coating. Oberst Hans-Joachim Kahler was in command of FGB. **Top and bottom right:** Mr Krier snapped the Panther again on 14 March 1947; the wrecked building has been demolished and a barn has been erected in its place. The Panther still rests in peace. **Lower left:** The Sturmgeschütz III from the previous page photographed on 14 March 1947. It has changed position, no doubt to clear the road, but the camouflage patterns match.

4x VDL(Krier)

Wrecks at Celles

Muzzle covers hang from 'Frieda' and her sister 15cm sIG33 as they stand sentinel between schwerer Panzerspähwagen of Pz.AA.2 at a collection point in Celles, Belgium. Hans Weber gets credit for breaking the 'code' of the tactical numbers : *"The PSWs still sport the pre-invasion tact numbers: 1152 = 1. Kompanie, 15. Trupp, 2. Fahrzeug. There were 12 troops (111-1122) with 'Pumas' (5cm)(Sd.Kfz. 234/2) and three additional troops 1131-1152 with the heavy stuff (7,5cm) (Sd.Kfz.234/3)."* Note that someone scrawled "BOOBY TRAP" on the stowage box of the 'Puma' on the opposite page. There is also a 'fence' on the engine deck of the Sd.Kfz.233, and it is unusual to see spare wheels carried on these recon vehicles. The German spearhead that reached Celles fell only a few miles short of the Meuse bridges. Celles then developed into a black hole that swallowed them, as British and American artillery, tanks and aircraft closed the pocket, knocking out the heavier Panthers and leaving the collection point to towed and wheeled equipment.

1x US Army via L.Archer, 2x NARA

Wrecks at Celles

Wrecks at Celles

The US 2nd Armored Division took Celles on Christmas Day, 1944, and some 'presents' such as this schwerer Panzerspähwagen (7·5cm) (Sd.Kfz.233) '1152' were still in the field long afterward. The vehicle belonged to 2.Panzer-Division and had a mix of 210-18 cross country tyres fitted, note the Trident insignia and tactical symbol for armoured car on front nose plate. With the side doors open on both sides, we can readily see what a thin shell of armour (14·5mm on the sides) these vehicles possessed. The elaborate railing on the side was there to protect the turn signal indicator and two small lights present on the earlier 8 Rad series. The soldier seen in the photo opposite may have been from the 3rd Royal Tank Regt of the British 29th Armoured Brigade. Cooperation between British and American forces was very good at Celles, with rocket-firing Typhoons playing a key role.

1x NARA, 1x L.Archer

Wrecks at Celles

Left and above: This le.Zugkraftwagen 1 t (Sd.Kfz.10) would have been near the upper levels of its towing capacity to draw a 1·4 ton 7·5cm Pak 40 through the hilly terrain of the Ardennes, although it was rated up to 1·8 t for the 15cm sIG33. Another vehicle would have been required to transport the Pak's ammunition. **2x NARA**

Opposite: A Steyr s.PKW, kl.Pz.Fu.Wg. (Sd.kfz.261), m.Fu.Pz.Wg. (Sd.Kfz.251/3) (note antenna on roof over co-driver and tip of 'Kurbelmast' in fighting compartment) and 2cm Gebirgsflugabwehrkanone 38 in Celles. **Above:** The crew of this vehicle could not be blamed for seeking shelter given the conditions in the Ardennes in the winter of '44-'45.

Bottom right: A de-fanged Selbstfahrlafette für 2cm Flak 38 (Sd.Kfz.10/5) with wider gun platform. Although DAK troops had complained as early as 1942 that the ammo boxes along the drop sides of the vehicle were susceptible to damage, they are still present here, as apparently no suitable alternative was found in the interim. **1x NARA, 2x L.Archer**

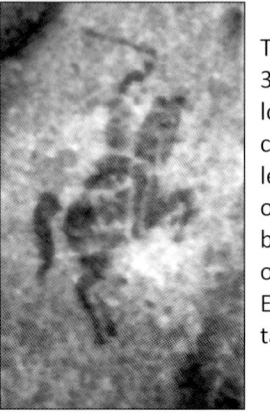

Tank '332', a Pz.Kpfw.IV Ausf.J from 3./Pz.Rgt.33, 9.Panzer-Division, looks as if it has come apart like a clown's car. This was the platoon leader's tank (Lt. Stenzel) knocked out on 14 January 1945. Lt. Stenzel bailed out unharmed. The insignia of Pz.Rgt.33 was the knight 'Prinz Eugen', seen here in front of the tactical number on the 'Schurze'.

4x NARA

At another collection point we find a 'Hummel,' a s.P.S.W. (5cm) (Sd.Kfz.234/2) and a rare Panzerbefehlswagen IV with a 1·4m T.S.R.1 ('Turmsehrohr') observation periscope mounted directly in the commander's cupola. (Note antenna base next to the cupola.) The mount consisted of an arm pivoted to a small bracket welded on the inner side of the cupola. A socket and clamp to accommodate the lower end of the T.S.R.1 is attached to the end of the arm. Driver's hatch propped up against front visor. **2x USAHEC, 2x NARA**

Opposite: A Panzerbefehlswagen IV (Sd.Kfz.267) covered by ETO Tech Intell Report #172 dated 8 March 1945 where it was erroneously referred to as an "*Observation Tank*" and the chassis number recorded as 92200. The turret roof has 'Pilz,' a ball mount for a T.S.R.1 observation periscope and a mount for a Fu 5 radio aerial where the 'Nahverteidigungswaffe' would be.
Above: The rear view shows the armoured 'pot' for the 'Sternantenne' on the rear hull for the Fu 8. This Fu 8 radio set was carried in the hull and the Fu 5 was carried on the right side of the turret. **Top right:** T.S.R.1 periscope. Note locking screw in base at the top of the turret, and the gun travel lock painted black. **Bottom right:** Base plate for GG400 auxiliary generator.   **4x NARA**

An anti-tank round, perhaps two, in the side of this Hummel has ended its days as a fighting vehicle. The 'Balkenkreuz' on the side has been obscured, but by whom, and why? Likewise a unit insignia has been painted over on the rear plate. The dark coloured mark near the end of the gun barrel is a wear mark from the gun travel lock, which itself has a German helmet on it. The 22 metric ton vehicle has started to sink into the ground.

2x L.Archer

A lonely looking 15cm sIG33 auf GW38(t) 'Grille' in Soller (Sonlez), Luxembourg. The most likely candidate for ownership is 9./Pz.Gren.Lehr-Rgt.901 or 902 from Pz.Lehr-Div who were in the area during January 1945. The distinctive large roadwheels have been removed, probably by locals. Part of the front armour of the fighting compartment is missing.

L.Archer

This combo of Jagdpanzer 38 and Bergepanzer III destroyed at Hosingen was first shown in Panzerwrecks 4. Hosingen was one of the routes used by German forces to retreat after the failure of 'Wacht am Rhein' so it is quite possible that the Bergepanzer had been towing the Jagdpanzer.

2x NARA, 1x L.Archer

Two civilians pose for a photo with a Jagdpanther from Stabskp. or 1./s.H.Pz.Jg.Abt.559 in Square Crépin, Rochefort. The tracks have been removed and are sitting in the background, this would have made moving the vehicle easier. Two vertical rows of spare track links are just visible on the side of the vehicle, under the thick blanket of snow. **L.Archer**

The III./Fhr.Gren.Brig. lost three of its eight Panthers during an engagement against troops of the US 319th Infantry Regiment, 80th Infantry Division at Dahl, Luxembourg on the morning of 8 January 1945. The Panthers were most likely assembled by Daimler-Benz, but the coat of whitewash has obscured all the markings. Fifty metres from the Panthers was a wrecked US M36 tank destroyer belonging to 610th Tank Destroyer Battalion. Civilians from Dahl later claimed that 19 tank wrecks were left in the area. **L.Archer**

Another of the Panzer wrecks at Dahl, this one a Jagdpanther from 1./s.H.Pz.Jg.Abt.519 destroyed at the crossroads on 7 January 1945. The Stab and 1 Kompanie of s.H.Pz.Jg.Abt.519 were equipped with Jagdpanthers, the 2. and 3. Kompanies were equipped with Sturmgeschütz III. The inset photo was the first to be taken and shows a full set of road wheels and camouflage materials, the main photo taken on 15 August 1945 shows that the roadwheels have vanished. **Right:** An inspirational vista, Panzerwrecks style.

1x MNHM, 2x L.Archer